Original title:
The Warmth Beneath the Frost

Copyright © 2024 Creative Arts Management OÜ
All rights reserved.

Author: Theodore Sinclair
ISBN HARDBACK: 978-9916-94-396-0
ISBN PAPERBACK: 978-9916-94-397-7

Surrendering to Ice

I slipped on ice while wearing skates,
A penguin passed, it had no mates.
My dignity went flying high,
As I flopped like a floundering guy.

The neighbors laughed as I took a spill,
My dog just stared, quite calm and still.
I'd wager he'd win the ice crown too,
For belly slides were all he'd do!

Rising with Fire

In winter's chill, I built a fire,
With marshmallows and jokes to inspire.
But who knew flames had such a knack,
For roasting my hair instead of the snack?

I danced around, what a silly sight!
The flames played tag, oh what a fright!
I yelled, 'Please don't take me with you!'
As my marshmallows turned into goo!

Flickers of Joy in a Silent Blizzard

A blizzard fell, all quiet and white,
Snowflakes danced, oh what delight!
I threw a snowball, missed my friend,
   And hit a tree, its branches bend.

The tree shook off its icy mantle,
Dropping snow on my face, oh the scandal!
We giggled loud, and forgot the freeze,
Making snow angels with utmost ease.

Hidden Flames in a Frost-Kissed Landscape

In frosty fields, I searched for cheer,
But all I found was snow and sheer.
Yet deep inside, a giggle lurked,
As frozen pants made me look quite jerked.

I hopped and skipped, a snowman's kin,
With arms of twigs, and a silly grin.
But when I fell, the snow flew high,
Nature laughed, oh how it did pry!

Nurtured Hearts in Frosty Embrace

A winter's day, we bundled tight,
With scarves and mittens, a cozy sight.
But tripping over a frozen log,
Made us both laugh 'til we were fog.

Our hearts warmed up, like tea in a cup,
As snowflakes kissed our cheeks, oh what luck!
In frosty breath, we sang and played,
And turned the cold to joy displayed!

Ember Threads Weaving Through the Snow

In winter's chill, the squirrels prance,
They wear their coats and take a chance.
With twinkling eyes and tiny toes,
They dance around in frosted clothes.

Snowmen boast their carrot crowns,
While giggles echo through the towns.
But snowballs fly like fluffy darts,
And tickle all the frozen hearts.

Glowing Spirits in a Frozen Labyrinth

Chilly winds bring icy fun,
Where snowflakes spin, and laughter's spun.
Hot cocoa waits on the stove,
With marshmallows dressed like little doves.

In snowmen comedies, laughter reigns,
As hats slide down in silly chains.
They wave their twiggy arms in glee,
Who knew cold could be so free?

Heat Rising From Icy Echoes

Frosty toes and noses red,
Chasing warmth in a sledding spread.
With every tumble and each fall,
We giggle like the merry hall.

Fire logs crackle with delight,
While snowflakes dance on a moonlit night.
We heat-make snow angels in the yard,
Their smiles joyfully never marred.

Smoke Signals in a Wintry Wilderness

Around the fire, we gather tight,
As stories fly into the night.
With hot dogs roasted and tales spun,
The icy grip can't weigh this fun.

As frost giants dance, we hold our ground,
With laughter echoing all around.
Their icy breath can't chill our cheer,
We crave the warmth that lingers near.

Beneath the Shimmer

Icicles dance like they've lost their way,
Snowmen plotting on a sunny day.
Frosty toes in a winter's prank,
Hot cocoa's smile, who'd need a tank?

Sleds scream down hills with joyful glee,
Penguins wearing caps, just wait and see!
With dashes of laughter, this winter's so bright,
Chilling with friends, what a silly sight!

Flames Resurge

In the fireplace, giggles and flames,
Marshmallows roast with ridiculous names.
The cat on a hotdog bun laughs just right,
As we toast to the sandwiches flying at night!

Socks on the radiators bring comic relief,
While the snowmen giggle, what's their belief?
Ice skates that slip but never lose style,
Sparkles of laughter, winter's best smile!

Heart's Whisper Warming the Frigid Air

With whispers of joy and puns in the chill,
We carve our dreams on the winter's white fill.
Snowflakes frolic, quite the funny crew,
Chasing hot air balloons that flew right through!

Pinecones wear hats, strutting with might,
While cocoa sneezes with a giggle of fright.
Polar bears juggling in fluffy ballet,
Who knew frosty days could bring such play?

Glows of Life Under Night's Frost

The stars giggle softly like they're in on a joke,
While frozen pizza dreams of being a smoke.
Snowflakes narrate tales that are sure to delight,
With elves doing pratfalls, oh what a sight!

Frost in the air tickles our nose,
While rabbits in sweaters strike goofy poses.
The moon moonwalks in pajamas so bright,
Winter's a party, oh what a night!

Frost-Kissed Echoes of Summer Days

Echoes of laughter ride on the breeze,
Recall summer's joy with a playful tease.
Snowballs like cannonballs splash with a cheer,
Who knew winter could be such a deer?

Ice creams are dreaming of sunny delight,
While snowflakes giggle, oh, what a fright!
With warmth in our hearts and socks on our feet,
We dance through the frost, oh, what a treat!

Searing Light in the Heart of Snow

In a land where cold is king,
Snowmen dance and winter sing.
Jack Frost tickles noses pink,
While penguins offer us a drink.

Frosty fingers wave hello,
As penguins try to steal the show.
Ice cream's a treat, but wait! Oh no,
It's just a block of freezing snow!

While icicles drip like frozen gold,
Snowball fights get brave and bold.
One slip, and down a friend will go,
Landing right in cold, white dough!

Yet beneath the icy quilt,
A party brews and laughter's spilt.
Warming hearts in snow attire,
With frosty fun, we'll never tire!

Bursting Buds Beneath the Winter's Shroud

Beneath the snow, a secret stirs,
Tiny green, like playful furs.
Cacti giggle, rain on their feet,
Mock the frost, and dance to beat.

While snowflakes swirl in wild delight,
A crocus dreams of spring in sight.
A garden gnome wears a frozen grin,
In winter's game, we all can win!

Pansies poke their heads with flair,
As squirrels play their winter dare.
With acorn hats and scarves from yarn,
They remind us it's quite a yarn!

So as we trudge through snow each day,
Hear laughter echo in the play.
Of buds and blooms, a song we sing,
Who knew the cold could also bring?

Ember Paths Through Frozen Forests

Through snowy trails where shadows creep,
Comes a light that makes us leap.
A campfire's glow amidst the trees,
Where marshmallows float like flurries tease.

Chubby raccoons, plotting like spies,
With giggles that spill out from their eyes.
They steal our snacks with sneaky grins,
In a game each laughter spins.

Beneath the frost, the embers glow,
Bizarre shadows dance in a row.
With hot cocoa brewed on the coals,
And stories shared, our heartbeats roll.

So let them laugh in chilly air,
While snowflakes twirl without a care.
Life's a joke wrapped in a freeze,
Finding warmth in frozen trees!

Warmth Lurking Beneath the Ice

Under the surface, giggles bloom,
Penguins in tuxedos dance in gloom.
They slide and glide, what a sight,
Wobbling like they're feeling light!

When snowflakes fall like cotton candy,
Little frosty friends get handy.
They build a fort, oh what a mess,
In winter's game, just to impress!

Icicles dangle, a great big tease,
They drip like jokes on chilly knees.
As we slip and trip in the freeze,
Winter fun comes with such ease!

So gather 'round this frosty night,
While chuckles warm with pure delight.
In the chill, we share the bliss,
A hearty laugh in winter's kiss!

Glimmers of Heat in Cold Shadows

In a world of ice, we dance and slide,
With snowball fights and winter's pride.
Frosty noses, cheeks aglow,
Who knew cold could spark such a show?

Tea kettle whistles, a joyful tune,
Hot cocoa swirls, a sugary boon.
Laughter erupts like a snowman's hat,
Who needs warm when you're snug as a cat?

Fingers frozen, yet spirits glow,
Every slip makes the fun grow.
In fluffy coats and muzzled shouts,
We chase the cold, without any doubts.

So here's to warmth in icy lands,
Where mittened gloves and snowflake bands.
Sipping joy from frosty cups,
Under the chill, the humor erupts!

Heartbeats Under Snow

Under layers of powdery white,
Laughter twinkles, a frosty delight.
Snowflakes spilling from a sneaky cheek,
Giggles burst like ice, so unique.

A penguin's waddle, a clumsy grace,
'Til frozen faces reveal a trace.
Shivering squirrels, plotting a craze,
They'll steal our snacks in crafty ways!

Hearts beating in this chilly place,
Winter's charm—a peculiar race.
While our toes may freeze in playful bliss,
In the cold, it's warmth we can't miss.

So let's create a snowman tall,
With a carrot-nose, we'll have a ball.
Dancing in boots, a joyful crew,
To the rhythm of winter's debut!

A Pulse in the Chill

A shiver and shake, fingers all numb,
Yet inside our hearts, the giggles hum.
Building castles made of frosty dreams,
Chasing snowflakes, or so it seems.

Frost on the windows, a crystal show,
But who cares? Just look at that glow!
Sipping cider by a fire's embrace,
While squirrels plot in their stealthy race.

Frost-kissed cheeks, so rosy and bright,
With a jump and a twirl, oh what a sight!
Wearing laughter like a cozy hat,
This chilly season's good like that!

So here's to the spark, the chuckle, the cheer,
In cold's tight grip, joy lingers near.
Where every slip is a reason to jest,
In the brisk of winter, we're truly blessed!

Melting Moments in a Frosty Landscape

With each flake that falls, a story unfolds,
Of chilly adventures and laughter bold.
Snowmen topple with a playful shove,
As we frolic through fields we dearly love.

Ice skating swirls, a wobbly dance,
Every fall brings a second chance.
Cheeks puffed out like little puffs,
Playing in snow is always enough!

Hot soup grins from a steaming bowl,
Telling jokes that warm the soul.
As the sun peeks, we celebrate,
With melting smiles, it's truly great!

So let winter's chill chase us 'round,
In every heartbeat, joy abound.
For under the ice, it's laughter we find,
A melting moment, one of a kind!

Whispers of Fire in a Frozen World

In a world so chilly, where snowflakes don dance,
Socks on the radiator, they take a chance.
The ice cream man shivers, his cart's stuck in place,
While penguins in parka contemplate life's race.

Hot cocoa's plotting an escape from the mug,
The marshmallows wanted a real cozy hug.
Snowmen with dreams of sunbathing on sand,
They scheme with the squirrels, a winter vacation planned.

Icicles sparkle, they're sharp as a knife,
A snowball fight now? Here comes trouble and strife!
The cat prances 'round like a furry old sage,
While mittens ignite with a feathery rage.

So gather your friends, the frost's not so mean,
For laughter can melt all the chill in between.
With joy as our fire, we'll dance through the snow,
In this frosty bazaar, let the good times flow.

Secrets of the Silent Earth

Beneath the white blanket, where hush whispers stay,
The ground hides its giggles in quite a sly way.
Mice wearing ski gear slide down on a hill,
While hedgehogs huddle for a group gossip thrill.

Bubbles from snowmen pop with a sassy delight,
As they gossip about the moon shining so bright.
The owls play poker by the old frozen pond,
Debating the merits of snow vs. abscond.

Flakes fall like confetti, the sky's got the flair,
While rabbits in top hats show off their best hair.
Each flurry a chuckle, each drift a good jab,
As snowflakes conspire to conquer and grab.

The whispers of secrets in winter's embrace,
Oh how they ignite with a soft, silly grace.
With frost as our canvas, let's paint it with glee,
In this frozen expanse, we're wild and so free.

Ember Hearts in Winter's Grasp

In the grip of the cold, where warmth hides for show,
A candle sings softly, its dance puts on a glow.
Chilly penguins quack with their frosty old cheer,
Swapping tales over cocoa, the joy's always near.

Frostbitten giggles echo through the bare trees,
The raccoons hold meetings by moonlight with ease.
A snowman's got jokes, and the icicles laugh,
As snowflakes line up for their group photograph.

Worms in a blanket, still snug in the dirt,
Whispering secrets that surely won't hurt.
Borrowed old thermals draped over thin air,
While frost takes the stage in a frosted affair.

The ground may be frozen, but hearts start to dance,
As warmth from our laughter gives winter a chance.
Let's toast to the chilly, embrace what we find,
In the frost of delight, our hilarity binds.

Beneath the Icy Veil

Beneath the hard crust where the secrets all lie,
The squirrels do yoga, they stretch to the sky.
Snowflakes parade like they own the whole street,
While rabbits make snow forts that can't be beat.

The frozen road sparkles with tricks up its sleeve,
As kids take a tumble, then jump up to weave.
Hot soup's a lucky charm in this icy domain,
Where laughter and warmth are the best kind of gain.

Coffee cups chatter, gossips with steam,
While marshmallows plot to create a sweet dream.
The ground is just frozen, but we melt it with cheer,
So let's fuel the laughter, let love be sincere.

For under the frost lies a humor so bright,
That dances through cold on a whim with delight.
In the cozy embrace of this thick winter freeze,
We'll warm up our hearts with each giggle and tease.

Laughter Hides in Winter's Embrace

Snowflakes giggle, dance on air,
Snowmen grinning, unaware.
Hot cocoa dreams in chilly hands,
Sipping smiles from snowy lands.

Icicles hanging like sharp teeth,
Froze a smile, but not my feet.
While penguins slide, I try to skate,
Fall on my face? Well, that's fate!

Chilly cheeks and noses red,
Lost my scarf, but found my bread.
Winter's chill can't take my cheer,
I'll laugh away, bring on the next year!

Under blankets, laughter's found,
Tickling toes, we huddle 'round.
The world outside is cold and gray,
But in here, we'll dance and play!

The Glow of Hidden Sunlight

Sunshine hiding in thick snow,
Like a prankster, I say, 'Hello!'
A warm sock puppet, a sight so funny,
Cold days melt with laughter's honey.

Outdoors I'm bundled like a burrito,
Tripping over boots, twirling like a veto.
Sledding down hills with giggly might,
Dreaming of spring with every flight.

Snowballs flying, what's the score?
Who knew snow could spark such war?
Whispers of warmth under frosty layers,
Fueling the joy of bold players.

As the sun peeks, we cheer and shout,
Winter's fun, there's no doubt!
We'll roast marshmallows, it's a must,
In laughter's glow, we place our trust!

Echoes of Comfort Amidst the Cold

Jingle bells and mittened hands,
Off to make snow angels in lands.
With rosy cheeks and cheeks that sting,
We laugh and shout, oh, what joy they bring!

A cat wrapped snug in knitted scarves,
Pretends it's tough, but bends and carves.
Let the winter festival commence,
With shadows of joy that make no sense!

Snowmen wobble with carrot noses,
Falling over, how funny it poses!
Chasing dreams in a chilly haze,
Hot chocolate laughter kinda sways.

Toasty fires with stories spun,
Echoing warmth, oh what fun!
With laughter shared and hearts so bold,
Joy thrives in every frosty fold!

A Hearth Within the Ice

Frosty windows, sights delight,
Fairies dancing in the twilight.
A whiff of pine, a crackling sound,
Silly elves prance 'round and 'round.

Woolly hats and mismatched socks,
Wearing snowflakes like feathered clocks.
We build a fire, our spirits rise,
Laughing as we burn my old ties!

Chasing squirrels in winter's maze,
Each slip and tumble, a laugh to raise.
The snowman whispers, 'Take a ride!'
He tumbles down, and so do I!

With every giggle, warmth is found,
Amongst the cold, our joys abound.
So gather 'round, let laughter flow,
A cozy heart, in chills, we glow!

Unseen Flames in Starlit Nights

In the snow, a squirrel does dance,
With acorns hidden, he's found a chance.
But oh! His tail, a snowy plume,
He thinks it's cool, but it's just his doom.

A snowman grins, with a carrot nose,
Wonders if he'll get to meet the crows.
With a scarf so bright and a hat so tall,
He schemes and dreams of a snowball brawl.

Penguins waddle, a silly parade,
All dressed up for a winter charade.
They slip and slide on icy ground,
A comical sight, oh what a sound!

Choco-lovers sip in cozy cafes,
While frost paints trees in curious ways.
They toast to joy, with marshmallows afloat,
In cups of cheer, let the laughter gloat.

Thawing Dreams Beneath a Glacial Sky

A whispered joke in the chilly breeze,
Brings laughter to life with the greatest ease.
Yet icicles hang like a frozen frown,
As snowmen schemed to take the crown.

Icicles chuckle; they're having a blast,
'Cause winter's fun is never outclassed.
A snowball flies, oh, what a flight!
It hits a dog who yelps with delight!

A frosty cake sits atop a hill,
Each slice a giggle, just for the thrill.
Sprinkles of snow on the frosting placed,
Even the birds can't help but be graced.

Under the stars, the fireflies glow,
Choosing winter just to taunt the snow.
They flash bright laughter, a twinkling glee,
While jolly old jokers sip herbal tea.

Flickers of Hope in a Frozen Tundra

A walrus wears a goofy grin,
In his tuxedo, he winks and spins.
With blubbery laughs on icy beds,
He dreams of fish tickling his heads.

Snowflakes sprinkle like scattered confetti,
On a polar bear getting all sweaty.
He rolls and tumbles, a fluffy blob,
Claiming he's here for the winter job.

A clever fox with a wagging tail,
Challenges birds to a laughing trail.
In snowball fights, they give it their all,
This winter's madness just beckons a brawl.

Yet as night falls, a snowman sighs,
With coal eyes sparkling under starry skies.
In frozen laughter, he dreams of spring,
Plus all the joy that the warm sun will bring.

Radiant Silence of the Cold Moon

Under the moon, a cat's diabolic plot,
To catch a snowflake or a steaming pot.
He leaps and bounds with a bootcamp flair,
Until he lands in a snowdrift; beware!

Frozen ponds reflect the giggles bright,
With skaters gliding in pure delight.
But whoops! One slips, oh what a sight!
A flailing dance under the soft moonlight.

The stars chuckle, a twinkling tease,
As snowflakes flutter like a playful breeze.
With every fall, they dance and spin,
In winter's game, they're bound to win.

So, raise your mugs, let's toast to the chill,
For every frosty thrill, we find our fill.
In laughter and joy, we'll always find,
A warm little spark that's truly divine!

Fragments of Heat in Midnight's Chill

In winter's grasp, we shiver and shake,
Dancing around for laughter's sake.
Hot cocoa spills, a comical scene,
Marshmallows dive like they're on the screen.

Socks on hands, fashion faux pas,
Snowball fights with soft, icy bwa-ha-ha!
Our noses red, like Rudolph's pride,
We giggle and stomp, hearts open wide.

Fluffy hats that seem out of place,
We roll in the snow, our frozen embrace.
Laughter ricochets, a joyful refrain,
In winter's chill, the fun won't wane.

Chasing snowflakes with silly zeal,
Wishing above for a white banana peel.
When frost bites back, we'll laugh and shout,
For silly moments, there's never a doubt.

Hidden Hearths in the Depths of Winter

Behind closed doors, we plot and scheme,
Building forts like a child's wild dream.
Cousins together, like marshmallows packed,
Who knew hot soup could bring such a whacked!

Fires crackle, with a pop and a hiss,
Our toast gets burnt, oh what a miss!
We hatch plans for a snow-day delight,
Jumping in piles till we reach new heights.

Mittens lost in the snowdrift's hold,
We search like detectives, truth be told.
And every time we find one pair,
We celebrate like we've struck gold so rare!

With snowflakes in hair, and cheeks bright red,
We argue who's winning in our snowball spread.
Under blankets, our giggles ignite,
In winter's embrace, all feels so right.

Hearts Ignited by Winter's Embrace

When snowflakes tumble and the world grows white,
We bundle up snug, ready for flight.
Wishing on stars that twinkle and glow,
For every slip on ice gives us quite the show!

Snowmen arise, with scarves oh-so bright,
Carrot noses, and eyes that are quite the fright.
We challenge each other to a dance in the cold,
Twist and twirl like legends of old.

Our laughter echoes through the frosty air,
As mittens disappear—yes, we lose a pair!
With every snowball that hits with a splash,
We savor the fun, forgetting the clash.

Hot soup awaits, bubbling and warm,
With humorous tales of winter's charm.
Cozy and soft, friends gather near,
In winter's hold, joy is always here!

Secrets of the Sun in Frosty Slumber

In blankets thick, we dream of the sun,
While sipping, we giggle, oh what fun!
The frosty breeze teases, whispers and snares,
Bringing forth shivers and laughter through flares.

Footprints left in paths snowy and bright,
Hot chocolate spills as we tilt it just right.
The puppet show starts, with snowmen as stars,
They dance with us under the moon's shining bars.

When icicles sparkle with joy in the air,
We imagine them melting—who would dare?
Sleds crashed on hills, with giggles galore,
In frosty adventures, we always want more.

As frost covers all, we find our sweet hub,
Sharing laughter and joy in the warm, cozy club.
Frosty secrets, we'll cherish through time,
In winter's embrace, every moment's a rhyme.

Beneath the Ice

Under the sheet, I start to slide,
A penguin grinned, with nowhere to hide.
He asked for a snack, I offered some fries,
He slipped on a peel, much to my surprise.

The cold air bites, but laughter flows,
As snowmen gossip, and winter glows.
A snowball fight breaks, full of cheer,
Dodging frozen peas flying near.

Shadows of Light Dance

Sunlight glimmers on icy traps,
Snowflakes jiggle like silly chaps.
They whisper jokes in the chilly air,
While squirrels chuckle, without a care.

Candy canes dangle from tree limbs thin,
As lights twinkle, their giggles begin.
The icicles melt with a goofy grin,
Each drop a chuckle, a frosty win.

Enkindled Souls Beneath Winter's Grasp

In the cabin, hot chocolate brews,
Plump marshmallows wear winter shoes.
They dive in cups, with giggly grace,
Swirling around in a frothy race.

A fire crackles, the logs fight back,
They pop and sizzle in a joyful flack.
With each leap, they take off their hats,
In a 'who's the best' game with the cats.

At the Heart of Frost

Chubby snowflakes tumble down,
One landed on my friend, the crown!
He laughed so hard, he fell right back,
  Creating a bumpy, snowy track.

Frosty windows paint funny scenes,
A snowman waving in floppy jeans.
The pets join in, all wagging tails,
  In this silly dance, no one fails.

Fires Flicker

Embers crackle with mischievous flair,
As shadows play games in the evening air.
A hot cocoa stirrer, well-versed in jokes,
Fireside knock-knock, with giggling folks.

Squishy socks shuffled on icy floors,
Rug burns show the paths of the whores.
Laughter erupts as we tumble around,
In the glow, funny tales abound.

Whispers of Warmth in a Snowy Stillness

In the stillness, whispers confide,
Snowflakes gossip, side by side.
They share old stories of groovy days,
When winter danced in quirky ways.

Polar bears slap their paws on the snow,
Racing each other, who'll steal the show?
With each tumble, snowmen cheer aloud,
In this frosty patch, we all feel proud.

Chasing Fires in a Wintery Silence

In the snow we dance and twirl,
Our mittens stuck in a snowy whirl.
Fireside chats about frozen toes,
Laughter erupts, and the warmth grows.

Hot cocoa spilled on my new white coat,
Racing snowmen, who can gloat?
Snowflakes land on my nose and chin,
While my dog plays fetch, he brings a win.

Hats askew, it's quite the sight,
Slip on ice, what a winter fright!
Still we giggle, through frozen fun,
Chasing fires till the day is done.

Though winter's chill tries to bring us down,
I'll take a slip, laugh, and wear a crown.
No chill can feast on my joy today,
I'll chase those blazes in the wild play.

Buried Light in the Grasp of Ice

Under layers thick like grandma's stew,
Lies a spark we always knew.
In this season of frigid stares,
We dig for laughter, and it repairs.

Snowball fights are quite essential,
Avoiding the cold? It's exponential!
We make our wishes on frost-kissed dreams,
While laughter bubbles in icy streams.

Huddled tight in oversized gear,
Who knew snowflakes could bring such cheer?
Laughter slides with frosty slides,
We'll dig for joy that winter hides.

Ice may grasp with hands so cold,
But here we find the warmth of old.
In the grip of winter's chill,
Our buried light is a manifold thrill.

Echoes of Warmth Wrapped in Chill

When the winds blow with frosty bites,
We wear scarves, look like weird flight kites.
Echoing laughter as snowflakes glow,
Who knew winter could steal the show?

Frosty cheeks and noses red,
In every corner, laughter's bred.
Frozen tummies from rolling down,
Yet smiling wide; we'll take that crown.

In fluffy jackets, we waddle like ducks,
Snowmen critiquing our building lucks.
With mittens stretched, we take a stand,
To embrace the chill with a giggling band.

From winter's grasp, we won't retreat,
With funny faces, this can't be beat.
We'll dance in ice, our joy won't spill,
In echoes of warmth, we find the thrill.

Soul's Glow in the Heart of December

When the world outside looks like a cake,
We bundle up and still partake.
Snowflakes twinkle with a playful tease,
In December's heart, we do as we please.

Puddle jumping, our boots all soaked,
Chasing shadows, with laughter we smoked.
Sledding trips that feel like flights,
Where we sprinkle joy in winter nights.

Mittens misplaced, winter's jest,
We chase after warmth; it's our quest.
Hot treats waiting, a sweet delight,
Cozy gatherings that feel just right.

In the cold, our spirits soar high,
Wrapped in giggles, we touch the sky.
In December's chill, our glow ignites,
In hearts of friends, the warmth ignites.

Frosted Petals on a Warm Breeze

I saw a flower in a mitten,
Its petals laughed, oh so smitten.
It shivered a tune, what a sight,
Underneath its frosty delight.

With frosted cheeks, it danced so bold,
Telling jokes that never got old.
A bee buzzed near, wearing a scarf,
He chuckled loud, it made me laugh.

What a strange world we have today,
When blooms get cold but love finds a way.
A sunflower tossed its seeds with glee,
'Catch me if you can!' it shouted free!

So here's to petals in snowflakes' arms,
Finding laughter in chilly charms.
They frolic and play, beneath winter's sigh,
Sprinkling joy as the days go by.

Secrets of Summer in Frostbitten Soil

The earth's a prankster, cheeky and sly,
Hiding sunbeams where cold winds sigh.
A squirrel in shades, on a frostbitten quest,
Searching for warmth, he never does rest.

Pockets of summer in frosty crust,
We dig for laughter, as we must.
'Is it spring yet?' we shiver and chatter,
Frosty secrets make our cheeks splatter.

Worms wearing earmuffs wiggle about,
They whisper sweet nothings, what a route!
'We're just a tad chilly, but who could know?'
As boots squish down, they start to glow.

So let's unearth those giggly rays,
Under frozen skies in comical ways.
For even when cold sends shivers and grunts,
Summer's just hiding, playing its stunts.

Bottled Suns in a Northern Sky

In the north, the suns are bottled tight,
Waiting for someone to sip them right.
A penguin made tea with a splash of glee,
Sipping sunshine, what a sight to see!

Snowflakes sprinkle down like confetti,
While frosty owls hoot, 'Ain't it pretty?'
Ravens in shades flock to a brew,
'Pass me that sun, and I'll share with you!'

Elves in the trees crack wise with glee,
Their wintery humor a sight to see.
A dog in a coat prances with flair,
Catching sun drops, while light dances in air.

Bottled suns twinkle, as night creeps in,
A warmth that spreads, where dreams begin.
So let us toast to the laughter we find,
In the chill of winter, where joy's intertwined.

Dreams Ignited Under a Frosted Canopy

Under a canopy of glistening lies,
Where snowflakes drop, and laughter flies.
A bear in a beanie roars with delight,
Telling stories of summer, all snug and tight.

Dreams are ignited with each frosty breath,
As squirrels scheme, plotting mischief and jest.
A snowman took selfies, flash on the go,
'Look at my scarf, it's all in the show!'

With icicles dangling like pipes of a band,
A choir of critters snaps up the stand.
They chant to the cold, with a wink and a grin,
'When spring rolls around, let the fun begin!'

So dance in the chill, let your spirit run free,
For frosted dreams will warm you, you'll see.
Under icicle chandeliers, bright and grand,
Life bubbles over in this winter wonderland.

Glow of Life Within a Frozen Expanse

In a land where ice skates roam,
Penguins party, making it home.
Snowmen dance with wiggly feet,
Chanting songs to the freezing beat.

Frosty smiles light the white streets,
While squirrels wear their warmest feats.
Hot cocoa flows like it's a race,
In this chilly, cozy place.

Mittens fly like kites in the air,
Catching snowflakes without a care.
Breezy whispers tickle the nose,
As laughter sparkles, winter glows.

Underneath, life hums and plays,
Jokes written in frosty displays.
For in this freeze, joy finds a way,
To melt our hearts, come what may.

Beneath the Crystal Blanket

Under ice, the rabbits joke,
Crafting snowballs that they hoke.
Chortles echo 'neath the sheet,
Of crystal blankets, oh so sweet.

Cold cheeks burst with laughter's spark,
As winter days embark on a lark.
Frozen trees wear coats of white,
Whispering giggles in the night.

In snowball fights, they take their stand,
With plans to conquer frozen land.
But oh, the snowmen strike back fast,
In a chilly duel meant to last.

Under the blanket, fun abounds,
While wiggly worms play on the mounds.
The laughter warms our icy hearts,
In this frosty land of playful arts.

Warm Dreams Dwell

In icy realms, where snowflakes dream,
Cookies bake in a cozy beam.
Jolly snowflakes hum along,
As playful winds sing a song.

Blankets piled in snuggly nests,
Winter's chill can't dim the zest.
Giggling hot chocolate spills,
Over mugs with marshmallow frills.

With snowmen tales that twist and turn,
They plot and plan, they laugh and yearn.
In dreams, they dance and prance about,
While chilly breezes twist about.

Underneath a frosty dome,
Tiny critters find their home.
In the cold, they play so brave,
Warm dreams thrive beneath the wave.

Heartbeats Cradled by Winter's Touch

When frost greets the blush of dawn,
Chipper critters prance on the lawn.
Flakes flutter down like joyful sprites,
Spreading chuckles through snowy nights.

Mittens squawk as they dance near,
While snowflakes tumble with much cheer.
Ice cream cones, oh what a twist,
Frozen delight that can't be missed!

Frosty noses wiggle with glee,
In this laughter-filled jubilee.
Who knew winter could be so bright,
With hearts that sparkle in the night?

And as the chill wraps all around,
Funny tales and frosty sounds.
Winter hugs with gentle squeeze,
While joy and laughter ride the breeze.

Flickering Memories in the Chill of Time

In the shimmer of icy glare,
Nutsy squirrels find treasures rare.
Mittens dancing in a spin,
Kick up snow, let the fun begin!

Snowball fights up on the hill,
Where laughter bubbles, never still.
Flashes of warmth in each frosty toss,
As knits and purls take a loss.

Gorgeous dreams clad in pale white,
Whirlwinds for our chuckling sight.
Memories warm like bacon and toast,
In this season we love the most!

With flickering joy that warms the heart,
Winter's chill can't keep us apart.
For in the cold, our smiles combust,
Creating warmth in frosty dust.

Vibrant Warmth Underneath

Beneath layers of ice, there's a glow,
A dance party for squirrels, don't you know?
They chat and groove in a flurry,
Who knew winter could be so merry?

Puddles of laughter, jokes cold as stone,
Snowmen cracking puns, they laugh alone.
With carrots for noses, they can't quite see,
The icy ball pit of their snowball spree!

Hot cocoa makes friends by the fire,
As snowflakes shake it like a live wire.
Marshmallows float, looking all so grand,
While penguins watch shows, all goofily planned.

Underfoot, the fun is yet to begin,
As snowball fights start, let the games spin!
So much joy hidden under the chill,
All's bright beneath the frost's frosty thrill.

Shadows of Summer in Winter's Grip

When winter's chill invites a fray,
The sun sneaks out for a brief play.
It whispers warm through frosted air,
"Tough it out, I'm almost there!"

The shadows of summer lurk with flair,
Like a sunbather in a winter chair.
With flip-flops on and a thick parka,
Beneath the snow, joys still spark-a!

While snowflakes fall, they sing a tune,
Dancing like summer under the moon.
Snowball fights turn into slip-and-slide,
As laughter echoes in winter's glide.

Hidden beneath all the icy fray,
Lies summer's giggle at winter's play.
So raise a cup and cheer with glee,
For warmth thrives here—just wait and see!

The Hidden Radiance of a Frozen Heart

In the land where frost meets the scheme,
Lies a heart full of joy, not just a dream.
Icicles glitter with laughter's cheer,
As winter's heart tries to shift a gear.

A snowman sighs, 'I'll make a friend,'
With twigs for arms that never bend.
His frozen heart is secretly bright,
In each chilly hug, winter's light!

Snowflakes tickle and laughter rings,
Funny hats and mittens, winter blings.
Underneath that chill, joy won't depart,
For comedy's pulsing in winter's heart!

So gather 'round, as the stories collide,
With puns so punny, they can't subside.
Long live the warmth where the ice tries to dart,
For giggles thaw even a frozen heart!

Frosted Reflections of Inner Light

In frozen mirrors, giggles gleam bright,
All bundled up, what a curious sight!
Frosted whispers from trees up high,
As winter chuckles in a snowy sky.

With snowflakes layered like stories told,
Laughter and warmth in the bitter cold.
Skating on ponds dressed in ice,
Falling with flair, not once thinking twice.

The sun winks down, making ice pop,
Mini snowmen chase, they just can't stop!
A frosty parade of mirthful delight,
Marching together—oh, what a sight!

Though chilly breezes may sway and swirl,
Inside each snowball, joy starts to whirl.
Frosted reflections of glee take flight,
While we laugh in the glow of the frosty light.

Secret Hearths in the Depths of Cold

In winter's chill, we find a spark,
A cat in a sweater, oh what a lark!
The firewood's stacked, not quite a big score,
But we'll roast marshmallows and ask for more.

The squirrels are plotting a nutty surprise,
While snowflakes dance down from the gray skies.
Wrapped in blankets, we giggle and cheer,
As we sip on cocoa, our lips disappear.

Frosty windows, a canvas of art,
A penguin invasion? It's just near the start!
We throw snowballs, but miss every time,
It's a comedy show, and we're in our prime.

So gather 'round, ye merry and bold,
For secret hearths keep us cozy and sold.
With laughter and warmth, let's make this a feast,
A winter's joke, with joy never ceased.

Radiant Heart in a Frostbitten Field

In a field of white, where snowmen loom,
A snowball fight brews, oh, let chaos bloom!
With carrots for noses, they dance in delight,
Yet one's lost an arm—what a comical sight!

The rabbits wear mittens, quite out of place,
While penguins audition for a silly race.
Frostbite may linger, but spirits stay high,
We're all a bit silly, and that's no lie!

A tale of a snow angel, not quite divine,
With wings made of snow, it's an awkward design.
The laughter erupts, as we tumble and roll,
In this frozen land, we're all on a stroll.

So raise your hot chocolate, let's cheer for the fun,
In this frostbitten field, we've already won.
With radiant hearts, we'll meet the cold glare,
For together, my friend, we'll conquer the air!

Beneath the Frosty Breath of Night

Under a blanket of shimmering white,
We chase the stars on this frosty night.
The moon's got a grin, shining bright on our backs,
While we skate on the ice, taking silly whacks.

A snowflake slips by, gets stuck on my nose,
It's a frozen tickle that nobody knows.
With mittens misplaced, and boots all askew,
We giggle and slip, what a comical crew!

The owls are hooting, they're throwing a bash,
As rabbits declare, "Oh, let's make a splash!"
With snowballs flying, it's a flurry of glee,
In this frosty breath, a wild jubilee.

So snuggle up tight in your layers and hats,
Let's dance through the night with our furry friends' spats.

For beneath the chill, there's laughter untamed,
In this wintery realm, we'll never be shamed!

Glimmers of Hope Under a Blanket of Snow

In a meadow so white, where mischief is found,
A mouse in a scarf stumbles over the ground.
With paws all a-flutter, it races a snail,
In this snowy wonderland, we'll never go pale.

Laughter erupts from the tiny snow forts,
Where penguins play king, and everyone courts.
With snowflakes like confetti, we throw up our arms,
In this wintry chaos, everyone charms.

The rabbits are giggling, in a dance so absurd,
While birds share their wisdom in nonsensical word.
A snowman debates with a nearby old tree,
About who tells the best jokes, oh what glee!

So gather around, let's toast to this cheer,
With glimmers of hope, we hold winter dear.
For under the snow, there's a festival bright,
Where laughter is king, and the cold's out of sight.

Beneath White Blankets

Snowflakes fall, a fluffy cap,
Hiding secrets like a nap.
Underneath, the world is still,
Squirrels dreaming, winter's thrill.

Laughter echoes through the drift,
Snowmen wobble, give a lift.
With each slip, a giggle springs,
Winter's fun, oh what it brings!

A snowball fight, a harmless war,
Puffed-up cheeks, we laugh and snore.
Dusting off our frozen gear,
Who knew naps were such a cheer?

So let the cold try to mislead,
Our hearts will dance like a speed.
Beneath the blanket, snug and tight,
We find our joy in the moonlight.

Life Awakens

Beneath the frost, the critters stir,
Tiny paws in playful blur.
Out from sleep, the world will peak,
With chuckles soft, the flowers speak.

Snowdrops nod, a funny sight,
Waking up with pure delight.
They tease the wind, a blooming race,
"Catch us fast!" they giggle with grace.

The bear in hibernation dreams,
Of honey jars and silly schemes.
Snuggled tight, with dreams so sweet,
He snores and rolls, a fuzzy feat.

As thaw arrives, the fun begins,
From frozen toes to sunny wins.
With each droplet, smiles will gleam,
Winter's jest, a merry dream.

The Stillness of Glowing Souls

Stillness hugs the world in white,
Cotton fluff hugs day to night.
Muffins warm, with cocoa clinks,
In silent joy, the kitchen winks.

Puppies prance in frosty air,
Chasing snowflakes, without a care.
Their funny snorts, as they dive,
In a snowbank where they thrive.

Tall trees don their snowy hats,
Standing proud like silly cats.
Branches shake with laughter's cheer,
As they whisper secrets near.

Underneath, a warm glow lies,
In every laugh, the sun will rise.
Though frost may chill, hearts will roll,
In the stillness, glowing souls.

Frosty Veils Over Fiery Spirits

Frosty veils dance on the lake,
Whispers of mischief, a playful flake.
Skaters glide with giggles wide,
As icicles cheer, they can't abide.

Mittens slip, and so does pride,
Who knew ice was such a slide?
With tumbles and a squeaky yelp,
Laughter spreads, no room for kelp.

The sun peeks out, a cheeky grin,
Melting walls where jokes begin.
From chilly mornings, warmth we chase,
In every joke, a wacky race.

Fireplaces crackle, stories spin,
Of frosty flops and goofy wins.
Though covered in a icy shroud,
Fiery spirits laugh out loud.

Secrets Unfurling in the Chill

Chill in the air, but spirits rise,
Swirling secrets beneath gray skies.
Snowflakes tumble, a comedy show,
As friends gather, with cheeks aglow.

Inside, the kettle sings a tune,
Hot chocolate dreams beneath the moon.
Marshmallows smile, a fluffy crew,
Who knew winter could be so true?

The garden waits, dressed in white,
Under the frost, it's a playful sight.
Seeds giggle, though silent they be,
Whispering of spring's jubilee.

In icy corners, laughter spills,
Through the chill, the heart just thrills.
With every secret winter keeps,
Comes laughter warm while the world sleeps.

When Solitude Warms the Soul

In a world of chilly sighs,
Laughter bounces off white skies.
Snowmen dancing, hats askew,
Frosty jokes are our debut.

Ice cubes freeze our drinks so nice,
Yet they melt with humor's spice.
Hot cocoa, laughter in a mug,
Leaves us all feeling snug!

Sledding down with squeals of glee,
Who knew winter's chill could be?
Fallen flakes become confetti,
In solitude, the joy is steady.

We share a grin, a snowball's flight,
Even penguins can't contain delight!
In this frosty fun parade,
The soul warms up, unafraid!

The Resilience of Fire Beneath Frosted Roads.

Beneath the frost, a flicker glows,
Dancing 'round as the cold wind blows.
Car tires spin, the ice won't crack,
But laughter leads us down the track.

Under blankets of white, we strut,
A sliding dance, in forms we cut.
Fear not the slip, embrace the fall,
For winter's fun can conquer all!

Fireside tales of warmth and whim,
Hot dogs roasted, spirits brim.
Snowflakes fight like tiny lights,
Silly battles, hilarious heights!

We revel in the chilly air,
With chuckles hidden in our hair.
So raise a toast to jokes and cheer,
For resilience thrives this time of year!

Embers Beneath Winter's Veil

A frosty morn, our breath a cloud,
We dance around, so silly, loud.
Each step a crunch, a winter tune,
Under the pale and watchful moon.

We warm our hands by silly flames,
Embers pop, like chatty games.
Witty quips fly like snowflakes,
In this chill, the spirit wakes!

From frosty lips, a joke is told,
While snowmen's secrets unfold.
With mugs of cheer, we raise our voice,
In winter's grip, we find our choice!

So gather 'round, don't miss the show,
With giggles wrapped in winter's glow.
We'll forge ahead and eat some pie,
For warmth is here, and so are we, oh my!

Hidden Glow in Icebound Dreams

In dreams of ice, a glow appears,
A hearty laugh replaces fears.
Slipping on a patch of frost,
We giggle, for our pride is lost.

Hidden treasures, snowflakes shine,
They twinkle bright for a sunny time.
Winter's magic dances near,
With punchlines that ring out so clear!

Every snowball hides a smile,
In coats too big, we play awhile.
With jokes as crisp as morning chill,
We laugh until we've had our fill!

So let the world be cold and gray,
For warmth persists in our own way.
With hearts aglow, we'll face the chill,
Together we shall laugh, we will!

Threads of Heat in Winter's Loom

In winter's quilt, we weave and stitch,
A dance of yarns, oh what a glitch!
The cats are tangled, the dog is free,
While we spin tales beneath the tree.

Fuzzy socks in mismatched pairs,
Knitting needles, tangled hairs.
Each loop a laugh, each knot a jest,
Fashion faux pas? We're feeling blessed!

Hot cocoa spills on the icy floor,
Laughter echoes, we always want more.
With every sip, the giggles rise,
Who knew a stain would bring such surprise?

So here's to warmth in our silly plight,
In frosty air, we'll share the light.
Together we stand with our frosty cheer,
Knitting love in the frosty sphere!

Beneath the Snow, Spirits Ignite

Snowflakes dance like goofy sprites,
Making snowmen, oh what sights!
But wait, what's this? A snowball fight,
Dodging mittens with all our might!

Frosty noses, cheeks aglow,
Chasing shadows in the snow.
Each slip and fall, a belly laugh,
Snowplow dreams on winter's path.

Hot soup brews in a pot so wide,
Who put the garlic? Oh, what a ride!
With every spoonful, tales unfold,
Of winter hiccups and moments bold.

So raise a cheer for snowmen tall,
And silly fights that end in a sprawl.
In frosty fields, we dance and play,
With spirits bright on a wintry day!

Flickering Stars in Frosted Air

Stars twinkle bright on a chilly eve,
Through frosted panes, we weave and weave.
Hot chocolate mischief, marshmallows fly,
Sippin', slurpin', oh me, oh my!

Carrots for snowmen, what a blunder,
They eat the hat, now how's that for wonder?
With laughter ringing through the frosty night,
In this silly realm, everything feels right.

With cheeks rosy red, and noses cold,
We share our stories, the young and the old.
Every grin a spark, igniting the dark,
Each flicker of joy, our winter's hallmark.

So raise your cup to this wintry scene,
Where laughter sparkles, bright and keen.
Under frosted skies with our hearts so light,
We find pure joy in the chilly night!

Radiant Seeds of Life in a Frozen Field

In fields of white, we plant a dream,
With snowballs flying, we're quite the team!
Seeds of laughter in drifts piled high,
The squirrels are giggling, oh my oh my!

With frostbit fingers, we craft a treat,
A cookie surprise, now that's hard to beat.
But wait, where's the sprinkles? What a shock!
The cat ate them all! Poor little flock.

Winter games, we stumble and fall,
Laughter echoing, we're having a ball.
With frosty breath and glowing cheer,
Each moment's a treasure, we hold dear.

So here's to the seeds we plant in the cold,
In fields of laughter, adventures bold.
With joy and mischief, this winter we'll thrive,
In frosty delight, we come alive!

Hearth of the Soul in Chilly Places

In a room where breath is steam,
The cat thinks it's a dream.
She curls up by the old pot,
Sipping cocoa, she's a lot.

The socks I wear are mismatched,
One has stripes, the other's patched.
But in the chill, they feel just fine,
Like cuddly food that's not a brine.

Mittens made of wooly glee,
High-fives from the nacho spree.
The dance of joy is quite absurd,
As I waltz with my frozen bird.

We laugh at snowflakes falling slow,
As they tickle our heads, we've got a show.
With cocoa highs and cocoa lows,
In chilly places, humor grows.

Whispered Ember in a Frozen World

A marshmallow floats, a fluffy boat,
In cocoa cups, we softly gloat.
The snowman's hat is down to his ears,
And he sneezes snowflakes, oh, what cheers!

The puppy trots in frozen glee,
Chasing icicles, what a spree!
He slips and slides like on a slide,
We laugh so much, we cannot hide.

In a world that glistens, ice and cream,
The chilly breeze becomes a meme.
We dance and twirl in goofy styles,
With hot cocoa mustaches, we tease and smile.

As icicles laugh, they chime away,
In this frozen land where we play.
The joy is warm, in every glance,
In the cold, we love to prance.

Beneath the Surface of Shimmering White

Under blankets, we hide from the cold,
Telling those stories that never get old.
The cat's got a crown, yes, she's the queen,
In this frosty world, she reigns supreme.

Our snowball fights are quite the sight,
Lobbing soft balls, oh what a fright!
We slip in the snow, and down we go,
Our laughter rings out in the winter glow.

With thoughts of cocoa and cookies too,
We make a plan, oh what shall we do?
A feast of treats beneath the sky,
With happy hearts as snowflakes fly.

The fun we have, it knows no end,
In chilly times, we laugh and mend.
For beneath the frost, our warmth will cheer,
In this silly world, winter's dear.

Flickering Shadows of a Frosty Dawn

Morning breaks, the sun peeks through,
Shadows dance, as they turn blue.
The squirrels gather, chattering loud,
While I sip tea feeling so proud.

My nose is red, like a cherry bright,
Stumbling out from cozy night.
The snowy landscape gives a giggle,
As I trip and do a funny wiggle.

Yet, warmth comes from laughter aloud,
Fueling the fire, we gather proud.
The chimneys puff like sleepy bears,
While we bundle up in the flares.

Each chilly breath reveals a grin,
In this frosty realm, let's dive in.
For flickering shadows, and hearts so bold,
Bring joy to the tale that winter holds.

A Flickering Flame in the Icy Depths

In winter's grip, I dance, oh so spry,
Doing the cha-cha while the snowflakes fly.
My socks are mismatched, my hat's on askew,
Yet here in the cold, I'm still feeling brand new.

A snowman joins in, he can't hold a beat,
With a carrot nose that's a bit too sweet.
But as we twirl through the frosty delight,
I swear I hear giggles from the stars at night.

The pond's frozen over, but my heart's a blaze,
Building a fire out of marshmallow gaze.
S'mores in the snow, now that's a great plan,
Icicles laughing, they think they're so grand.

With snowball fights ready, we laugh and we cheer,
Life is a party, come grab a warm beer!
So when winter bites, I'll just shiver and grin,
In my frosty dance, let the fun begin!

Whispers of Heat in a Winter's Tale

Once a penguin, sleek in a furry tux,
Told jokes to polar bears, oh, what quirky bucks!
'Why don't you ever see a snowman at play?'
'Because they melt down at the end of the day!'

In a world full of snow, call it winter's court,
We have hot cocoa and marshmallows for sport.
Sipping on laughter, a festive delight,
With snowflakes that sparkle like stars in the night.

Elephants skied, with trunks waving all around,
Sledding on candy canes, oh joy profound!
So when the chill brings a smile to my face,
I know winter's humor holds a special place.

Where frostbites are jokes and icicles gleam,
We're all just warm hearts caught up in a dream.
So let the north wind play its icy tune,
I'll waltz with the snowflakes, beneath the moon.

Beneath the Chill, a Luminous Heart

Snowflakes are fancy, each one's wearing a hat,
While my nose turns red, just like my pet cat.
The chilly air tickles, I giggle and spark,
Who needs a fireplace when you've got light in the dark?

Beneath all this ice, a secret dance lies,
With snowmen busting moves, quite the surprise!
They twirl and they spin, with a carrot ballet,
Just waiting for spring to join in the fray.

My dog wears a sweater, it's uniquely insane,
He prances in circles, embracing the rain.
Puddles of laughter, and giggles galore,
Winter's a party, who could ask for more?

So let's toast to the frost, with a cup of hot tea,
Life's a warm comedy, come dance with me!
With each chill that bites, we'll chuckle and cheer,
For the warmth in our hearts is forever sincere.

Dreams Buried Under Ice

In a land where the snow likes to pile up high,
The penguins are plotting, oh my, oh my!
With ice skates on flippers, they glide with such grace,
Looking for warm cookies, a sweet little chase.

Under mountains of frost, the marshmallows play,
Making snow angel shapes, in a sugary way.
But oh, what a sight, when the cookies go round,
Snowmen get jiggly, with laughter abound!

A squirrel in a scarf is roasting a nut,
Declaring he's king of this chilly little hut.
His subjects all giggle, with cocoa in hand,
Caught in this glee, who could possibly stand?

With dreams buried deep, where the icy winds swoosh,
Our hearts stay aglow, in a wintery hush.
Life's filled with humor, in snowflakes aglow,
As we dance through the cold, embracing the show!

Glow of Memories in a Snowy World

In a land where snowmen stand too tall,
Their carrot noses droop, they stumble and fall.
The whispers of winters tickle our ears,
As we laugh 'bout hot cocoa, swapped for cold beers.

Sleds zoom past, while penguins take a seat,
They slide on ice, achieving quite the feat.
With snowballs flying, aimed at my hat,
I duck and I dodge, but may just fall flat.

Snowflakes spark joy, like confetti in flight,
Each one a giggle, from morning till night.
Memories coated in fluffy white dust,
Reminding us laughter is surely a must.

So bundle up tight, let the fun all begin,
With stories of snow, we'll dance and we'll spin.
For the chill in the air is no cause for dread,
When carrying warmth, that's all in your head.

Fireflies Dancing in the Frost-clad Night

Once in a winter, on a frosty march,
Fireflies waltzed in a dance, quite the arch.
Wearing tiny mittens, they twirled with glee,
As snowflakes joined in, a rare jamboree.

Icicles hung like chandeliers so grand,
While critters slid in unplanned bandstand.
With a swish and a swoosh, they slipped and they fell,
In the chill of the night, it rang like a bell.

Our noses are red from the cold winter air,
Yet laughter ignites, like a bonfire's flare.
We'll dance with the fireflies, brave and so bold,
In a frosty ballroom where stories unfold.

So come join the fun, don't mind the chill,
For in every snowflake, there's magic until,
We warm up our hearts, like stars in the sky,
Laughing 'til morning, oh my, oh my!

Beneath Each Flake, a Heart Breathes

Under the blanket, the snowflakes reside,
Buried in giggles, where secrets can hide.
Each flake a reminder of joy's lovely game,
With snowmen that chuckle and whisper your name.

Snowball fights break out in the absence of peace,
Bringing forth chaos, yet granting release.
As frost bites our noses, we proclaim with cheer,
'Pass me the marshmallows, we've nothing to fear!'

With each crunch and crackle beneath winter's shoe,
Are whispers of laughter and tales that ensue.
So let's sip on our cocoa, add some more cheer,
For the spirits of winter sing sweet in the clear.

So dance through the drifts, let snowflakes ensnare,
In the whirlwind of joy, there's no room for despair.
Life's a frosty adventure, just give it a chance,
With love in the air, it's a magical dance.

Warmth Encased in the Winter's Breath

When chilly winds blow and the frost starts to bite,
A snowman is born, dressed in pure white.
With a hat and a scarf, he struts down the lane,
But his nose is too bright, it drives him insane.

Gather 'round fires with blankets in tow,
Tell tales of the flurries, the fun times we know.
While sipping hot chocolate, we can't help but smile,
It's the little things, like snowmen's style.

Dance in the streets as the snowflakes do fall,
With hats on our heads, we're ready for it all.
Snow angels and laughter, our wintertime cheer,
Each frosty encounter, a memory dear.

So here's to the laughter, with cheeks ever red,
In dreams filled with winter, we'll always be led.
To the heart of the season, where glee never ends,
And in every good snow, a soft giggle blends.

Soft Firelight in a Frosty Hollow

In a hollow where chill winds blow,
A flicker plays, putting on a show.
The snowmen dance with cheeky grins,
While squirrels sip cocoa, wearing chins.

A marshmallow's plight, it floats away,
On laughter's breeze, it starts to sway.
The ailing log rolls over with glee,
It's just too hot—wait, is it me?

As icicles twinkle like disco balls,
Hot chocolate spills, oh how it sprawls.
Frosty faces all aglow,
In this sweltering winter's show.

So gather 'round this cozy cheer,
Forget the chill, unwind, my dear.
In the frosty night, we find delight,
With fire's embrace, oh what a sight!

Silent Heat Amidst Icy Whispers

Silent whispers among the flakes,
The snowflakes giggle, making mistakes.
A snowball fight that's quite the sight,
Turns into laughter well into the night.

Melting snowmen, they start to frown,
One sad carrot nose falling down.
They gather close, share jokes, and laugh,
Their frosty tears become a bath.

Beneath the frost, a little heat,
As penguins frolic on a slipping seat.
They twirl and slide, all full of cheer,
Who knew that winter held such queer?

So raise a cup to frosty fun,
While the chill outside has just begun.
In silent heat, we break the cold,
With silly tales just waiting to be told!

Cinders of Hope in a Winter's Night

Under the stars, the embers glow,
A flame flickers—where'd it go?
The logs have a plot twistingly funny,
As they tell tales of summers sunny.

Frost nips at toes, a chilly jest,
But cinders spin stories, giving their best.
With marshmallows popping like giggles loud,
The joy of winter makes us all proud.

S'mores collapse, oh what a sight,
A gooey mess, but feels so right.
The frozen air, so crisp and clear,
Holds laughter tight, banishing fear.

Each spark that dances among the peanuts,
Turns winter's cold into warm feats.
For in this night of frosty delight,
The cinders of hope shine ever so bright!

The Hidden Glow of a Frosty Muse

Beneath the ice, a secret lies,
A frosty muse with shimmying thighs.
She hums a tune to the icy stars,
While penguins chuckle, smoking cigars.

Snowflakes swirl with a giggling breeze,
Waltzing around like they own the freeze.
With hidden glow in every flake,
They sing of warmth—make no mistake!

So grab your mittens, let's have a laugh,
As frost bites the air, on our warm path.
A hot cup spills, we all slip and slide,
In this frosty delight, our spirits glide.

With each little spark, we brighten the night,
A magical scene, oh what a sight!
The hidden glow winks through the chill,
Winter's a canvas that warms at will!

Beneath the Chill

In jackets thick, we bundle tight,
With ice cream cones that freeze mid-bite.
Snowflakes dance, they tickle our nose,
Hot chocolate spills as laughter flows.

The penguins watch with beady eyes,
We slip and slide, oh what a surprise!
Winter games, such silly fun,
Who knew chill could be so run?

Sledding down the hill with glee,
The snowman waves – not one, but three!
Inside we roast our marshmallow dreams,
With goofy jokes and silly schemes.

The cold can try to bite and freeze,
But warmth from friends is just the tease.
Laughter bubbles, it fills the air,
Under the chill, we have no care.

Flames Await

The firewood's stacked like a game of Jenga,
One wrong move and it might just end ya.
We dance around with flames' wild cheer,
Hot dogs roast, we all lose fear.

In thick wool socks and slippers bright,
We twirl like penguins, what a sight!
The embers crackle, a warm delight,
Sharing silly tales all night.

Sipping soup that's piping hot,
The cat's in there, oh did he spot?
Lurking close for food on the go,
Each bite a laugh, a funny show.

Though frost bites toes and cheeks so red,
We'll pop our popcorn, squash the dread.
With laughter echoing, the flames do play,
Our hearts are bright on winter's gray.

Silent Melodies of a Hidden Hearth

In quiet corners, the stove's a star,
With pots that bubble, oh so bizarre.
Charcoal cookies, what a flop,
Yet we chuckle, we'll never stop.

Neighbors peer through frosted panes,
What's that smell? Oh, we have no claims!
Songs of crackling, sweet serenade,
With mistletoe dreams, we dance unafraid.

Baking fails lead to giggles bright,
Icing disasters, a comical sight.
We gather 'round with spoons in hand,
Who needs a feast when fun's so grand?

The heat's a secret, we'll never tell,
What really happened? Oh, it's just swell!
With love and laughter, the hearth stays warm,
In frost's embrace, we form our charm.

Glow of Life Amidst Icy Sighs

Frosty windows, art made in breath,
A canvas of chill, but no sign of death.
Our wild snowball fights, like ninja spies,
Laughter fills the air, no need for lies.

With hands warmed by mittens, we dash about,
Chasing our dreams, we spin and shout.
A banana peel lies, fate does conspire,
Down goes a buddy, rolled like a tire!

But oh, the glow from within the den,
Where giggles echo again and again.
Sipping drinks, marshmallows afloat,
These moments are gems, we happily gloat.

So let winter's breath frost our cheek,
In silly dance, we find what we seek.
In frigid nights, love's warmth will rise,
Life's laughter dances, none can disguise.

Veins of Heat Beneath the Winter's Skin

Under thick layers and cozy purls,
We're bundled like burritos, yet still we twirl.
Snowflakes fall on our noses and lips,
As neighbors throw snow, and laughter trips.

A snowman looms with a lopsided grin,
While snowballs fly from our heads to chin.
Each frozen tumble a tale to tell,
In the winter's chill, we know it so well!

Hot cider steaming, fingers all stuck,
With mittens on wrong, oh what's our luck?
Yet songs of joy spill from each heart,
In cozy corners, we play our part.

So let it snow, we'll laugh through the chill,
With warmth in our souls, we'll climb every hill.
For beneath each cold, a funny surprise,
In every frosty breath, joy never dies.

Milton Keynes UK
Ingram Content Group UK Ltd.
UKHW022143111124
451073UK00007B/175

9 789916 943960